D0778721

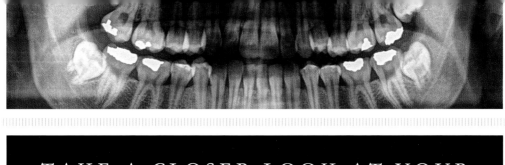

TAKE A CLOSER LOOK AT YOUR
Teeth

BY JENNY FRETLAND VANVOORST

The Child's World

Published by The Child's World®
1980 Lookout Drive • Mankato, MN 56003-1705
800-599-READ • www.childsworld.com

Acknowledgments
The Child's World®: Mary Berendes, Publishing Director
Red Line Editorial: Editorial direction and production
The Design Lab: Design
Content Consultant: Jeffrey W. Oseid, MD

Photographs ©: Evgeny Karandaev/Shutterstock Images,
title, 19; Brand X Images, title, 23; Shutterstock Images, title,
7, 9, 17, 18, 24; Monkey Business/Thinkstock, 5; Hemera/
Thinkstock, 11; Vectomart/Shutterstock Images, 13; Alila Sao
Mai/Shutterstock Images, 15; Jupiterimages/Thinkstock, 21

Front cover: Brand X Images; Shutterstock Images; Evgeny
Karandaev/Shutterstock Images

ISBN: 978-1623235550
LCCN: 2013931444

Printed in the United States of America
Mankato, MN
July, 2013
PA02175

About the Author
Jenny Fretland VanVoorst is a writer and editor of books for young people. She enjoys learning about all kinds of topics and has written books that range in subject from ancient peoples to artificial intelligence. When she is not reading and writing, Jenny enjoys kayaking, playing the piano, and watching wildlife. She lives in Minneapolis, Minnesota, with her husband, Brian, and their two pets.

Table of Contents

CHAPTER 1

What a Mouthful!

Teeth help you eat. They also help you smile and speak. You probably don't think about your teeth a lot. Your teeth stay busy helping with digestion and communication. Your teeth have an important role in your daily life.

The words "dental" and "dentists" come from the root word *dent*. This means tooth in Latin.

Chewing is the first step in the digestive process. This process begins when you take a bite of food. Your teeth cut and grind food into smaller pieces. These pieces travel to your stomach, where they are digested.

Your teeth cut your food into small pieces before it travels to your stomach.

Teeth come in many different shapes. The tooth's shape helps it do its job. The four front teeth are called incisors. Incisors are on both the top and bottom jaws. These sharp teeth are made for cutting up food. On either side of the incisors are pointy teeth called canines. These teeth are like a dog's sharp fangs. In fact, canine is the Latin word for "dog." Canine teeth tear food into smaller pieces. There are two canine teeth on the top jaw and also on the bottom jaw.

After the canine teeth are the premolar teeth. These teeth are wider and have a flatter top. There are eight premolar teeth. Behind the premolar teeth are the molars. The molars are wider and flatter than the premolar teeth. Molars are used to grind food.

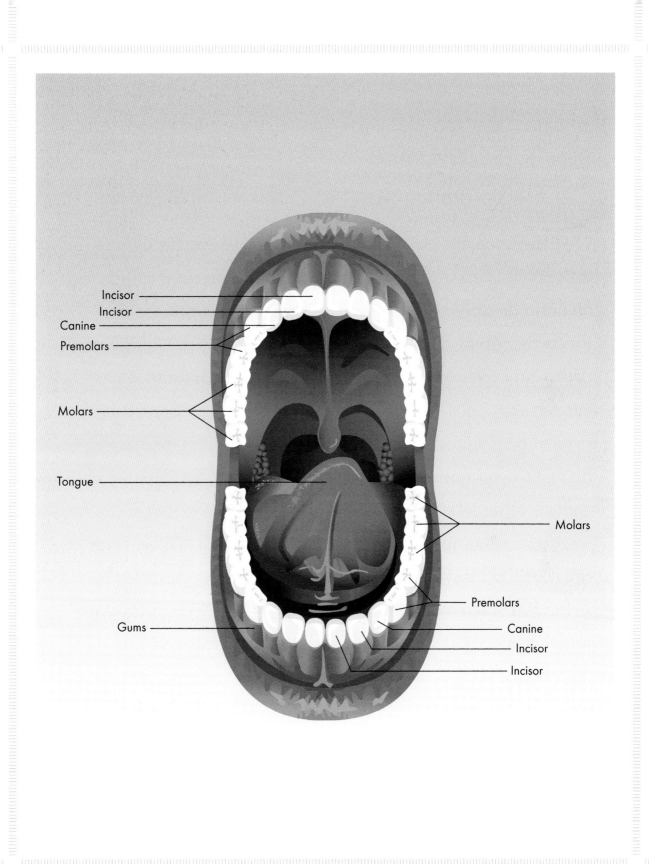

Your teeth are great for chewing, but you also need them to talk. Your teeth work with your tongue and lips to form sounds. You could not say "tooth" correctly without your teeth. The tongue needs the front teeth to make the "th" sound. Without your teeth, the word would come out sounding like "toof."

Teeth help you talk so people can understand you. Teeth also help you communicate in other ways. The meaning behind a smile is always clear!

Teeth help you talk and smile!

CHAPTER 2

Getting to the Root

Most babies are born without teeth. Teeth start to come in when a baby is about six months old. By two years old, most kids have a full set of 20 teeth. These are called baby teeth.

Some adult animals, such as sharks, regrow teeth when they lose them. Humans have only one set of adult teeth. If you lose an adult tooth, it is gone for good.

Baby teeth are not permanent. As the body grows, so does the mouth. This makes room for more teeth in the mouth. Baby teeth are pushed out and replaced by permanent adult teeth. Most kids will have 28 permanent teeth by 12 years old. There are four other molars that could grow in. These molars are called wisdom teeth. Not everyone grows wisdom teeth. Adults with wisdom teeth have a full set of 32 teeth.

As you get bigger, your adult teeth will replace your baby teeth.

Let's get to the root of these 32 chompers. The outer part of a tooth is called the **crown**. It is the part everyone can see. You chew, smile, and talk using the crowns of your teeth. The crown is covered in a hard material called **enamel**. Enamel is the hardest material in your body. It is even harder than your bones! Enamel protects your inner tooth from the wear and tear of chewing. It also protects teeth from hot or cold. Without enamel, eating ice cream or drinking hot chocolate would be painful.

The crown covers a layer of bone-like material called **dentin**. Dentin surrounds and protects a soft inner **pulp**. The pulp contains a tooth's blood vessels and nerve endings. Blood vessels carry nutrients to a tooth. Nerves send messages to the brain warning of tooth problems. Pay attention to these messages. It is easier to fix a problem if you catch it early.

Your teeth are set into your jaw by roots. Front teeth have a single root. Molars have two or three roots. Gum tissue wraps around your jaw and the roots. It helps hold your teeth in place.

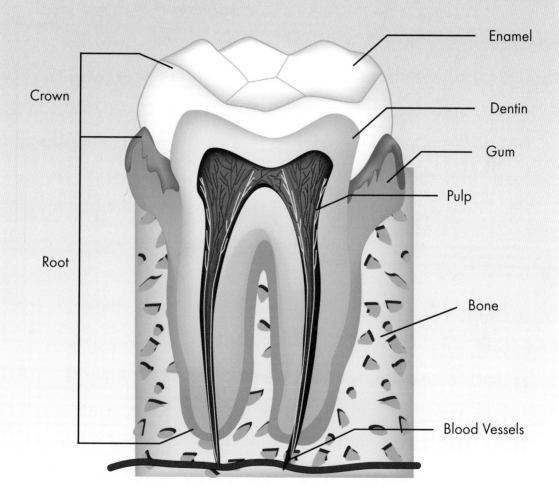

Crown

Root

Enamel

Dentin

Gum

Pulp

Bone

Blood Vessels

CHAPTER 3

When Good Teeth Go Bad

There is a lot going on in your mouth. **Bacteria** in your mouth are always looking for a good meal. Bacteria feed on scraps of food stuck between your teeth. As they feed, bacteria multiply. They group together to form a material called **plaque**. It sticks to your teeth and makes an acid. The acid eats through the enamel and causes the tooth to rot.

Over time, coffee, tea, foods, and medicine can stain enamel. That's why young people's teeth are usually a brighter white than those of adults.

This rot creates a hole in the tooth. It is called a **cavity**. Cavities are a common tooth problem. They are usually easy to fix, too. The dentist removes the infected part using a drill. Then the dentist fills the area with a material called **porcelain**. The porcelain blends in with the teeth. Some people get cavities more easily than others. Most people will have at least one cavity.

The stages of tooth decay

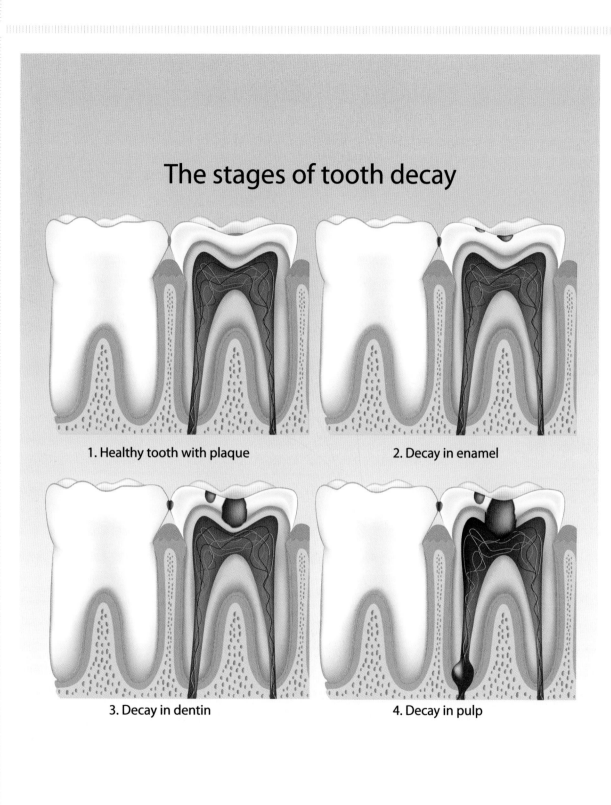

1. Healthy tooth with plaque

2. Decay in enamel

3. Decay in dentin

4. Decay in pulp

Sometimes bacteria grow into the **gums** and attack gum tissue. This causes the gums to pull away from the teeth. It also creates a space where more bacteria can live. The problem becomes worse when this happens. Gum disease is more common in adults than children. Brushing the teeth more thoroughly and gently can treat gum disease.

Teeth do not always fit the mouth they are in. They can be crowded or crooked. Teeth might not line up properly. This might make it hard to chew food or awkward to smile much. Special dentists called **orthodontists** work on these problems. They may suggest wearing braces. These metal devices attach to the teeth and gently pull them together. An orthodontist may also remove teeth. This will give crowded teeth extra space.

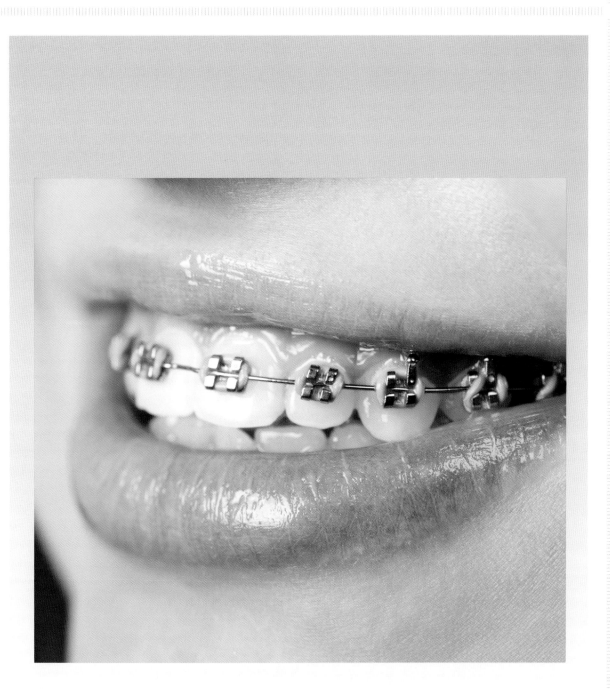

Braces help straighten crooked teeth.

If an adult has wisdom teeth, they are often removed. Wisdom teeth cause problems when there is not enough space. It might be hard to fit four new teeth. Wisdom teeth also do not always come in straight.

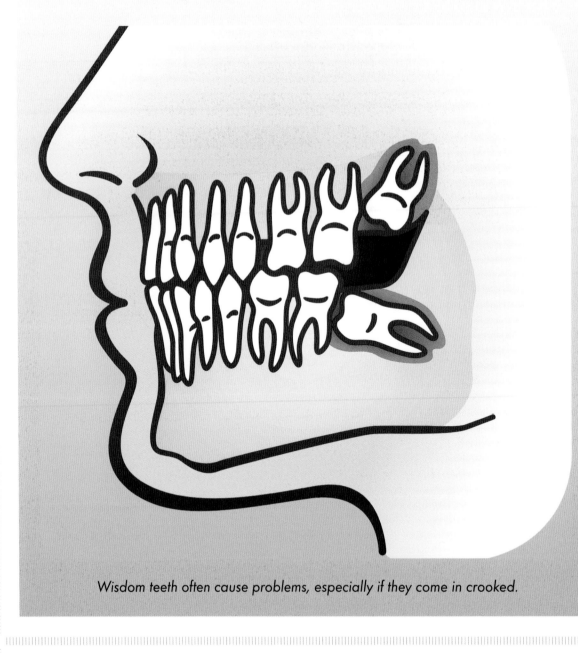

Wisdom teeth often cause problems, especially if they come in crooked.

Most tooth problems can be avoided with simple dental hygiene. Taking good care of your teeth will keep your smile healthy.

Your toothbrush helps you take good care of your teeth.

CHAPTER 4

Brush Up on Dental Care

Let's brush up on dental care. The best tool for preventing tooth problems is your toothbrush. Choose a brush with soft bristles. They are the gentlest on your gums. Brush your teeth twice a day. Use toothpaste with fluoride, a mineral that strengthens tooth enamel. Make small circles over your teeth with your toothbrush. You should spend about three minutes brushing. Don't forget your back teeth! Use dental floss to clean the areas between your teeth.

Before toothpaste was invented, people used ashes or chalk to clean their teeth.

Food can have an effect on your dental health, too. Avoid candy and other sweets. Sweet foods cause more tooth decay than other foods. Brush right away after eating something sweet. Calcium helps keep teeth strong. Instead of sweets, eat foods like dairy products.

Visit a dentist twice a year. A dentist will check your teeth to catch any problems early. He or she will also clean your teeth. The dentist's special tools make your smile bright and sparkly.

Take care of your teeth. Your smile will last a lifetime!

Brushing is the most important way to keep your teeth healthy.

GLOSSARY

bacteria (bak-TIHR-ee-uh) Bacteria are microscopic living things that are all around you. Bacteria in the mouth can lead to gum disease.

cavity (KAV-uh-tee) A cavity is a hole in something solid. Most people will have a tooth cavity before they are teenagers.

crown (KROUN) The crown is the top of something. A tooth's crown is covered by enamel.

dentin (DEN-tin) Dentin is the tooth material that surrounds and protects the pulp. The crown covers the dentin.

enamel (i-NAM-uhl) Enamel is the hard, white surface of your teeth. Enamel is the protective material that covers the whole tooth.

gums (GUHMS) The gums are the areas of pink flesh around the teeth. Gums help bind teeth to the jaw.

orthodontists (or-thuh-DON-tists) Orthodontists are dentists who straighten uneven teeth. An orthodontist may put on braces to fix crooked teeth.

plaque (plak) Plaque is the coating made from food and bacteria. Plaque sticks to teeth and can make an acid that harms teeth.

porcelain (POR-suh-lin) Porcelain is the hard material used to fill dental cavities. Porcelain blends in with the tooth.

pulp (PUHLP) Pulp is the soft inner part of the tooth. Pulp contains blood vessels and nerve endings.

LEARN MORE

BOOKS

Ferguson, Beth. *Teeth*. New York: Marshall Cavendish, 2004.

Miller, Edward. *The Tooth Book: A Guide to Healthy Teeth and Gums*. New York: Holiday House, 2009.

WEB SITES

Visit our Web site for links about the teeth: **childsworld.com/links**

Note to Parents, Teachers, and Librarians: We routinely verify our Web links to make sure they are safe and active sites. So encourage your readers to check them out!

INDEX

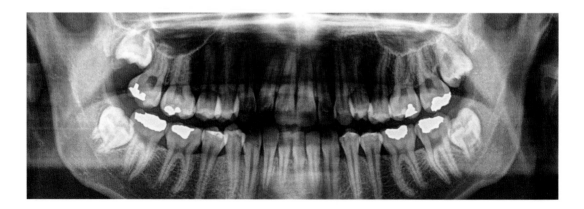